Watch It Grow
Ladybird
Barrie Watts

FRANKLIN WATTS
LONDON•SYDNEY

First published in 2004 by Franklin Watts
96 Leonard Street, London EC2A 4XD

Franklin Watts Australia
45-51 Huntley Street, Alexandria, NSW 2015

© Barrie Watts 2004

Editor: Kate Newport
Art director: Jonathan Hair
Photographer: Barrie Watts
Illustrator: David Burroughs

A CIP catalogue record for this book
is available from the British Library

ISBN 0 7496 5429 5

Printed in Hong Kong, China

How to use this book

Watch It Grow has been specially designed to cater for a
range of reading and learning abilities. Initially children may
just follow the pictures. Ask them to describe in their own
words what they see. Other children will enjoy reading the
single sentence in large type, in conjunction with the pictures.
This single sentence is then expanded in the main text. More
adept readers will be able to follow the text and pictures by
themselves through to the conclusion of the life cycle.

Contents

Ladybirds come from eggs.

Ladybirds are **insects**. They have six legs, a pair of wings and two small eyes.

The female ladybird lays tiny eggs on the underside of a leaf. This is to shelter the eggs from the weather. The eggs also have a tough skin, to stop them from drying out.

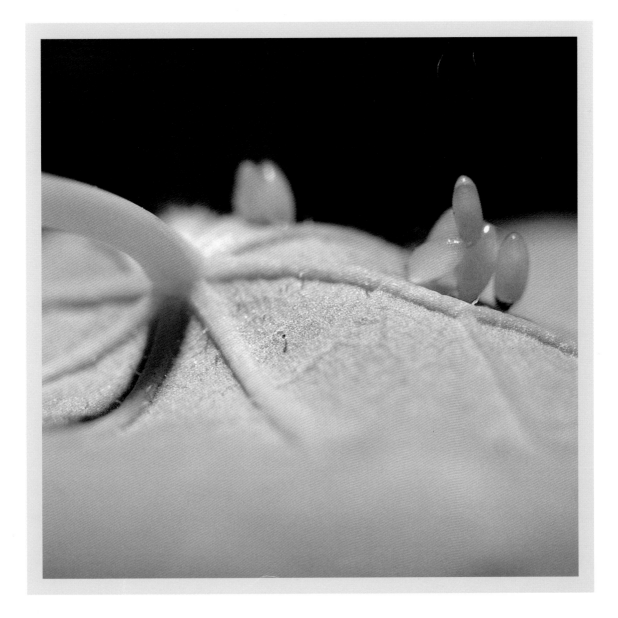

The female lays her eggs.

In spring, the female lays the eggs in **batches** of up to 50 eggs at a time. After three days, the eggs change colour.

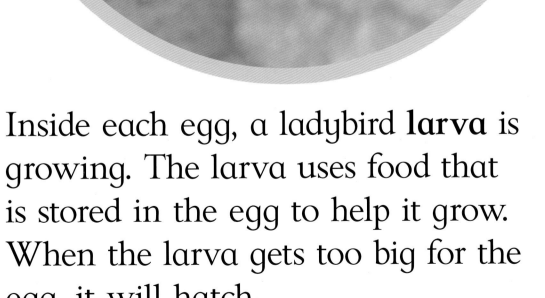

Inside each egg, a ladybird **larva** is growing. The larva uses food that is stored in the egg to help it grow. When the larva gets too big for the egg, it will hatch.

The eggs hatch.

After five days the **larvae** split their shells and crawl out. They are about as big as a pinhead. They stay in a group until their damp skin dries out and hardens.

After they have rested, the larvae need to find food. Their jaws and mouth are hard now, so they can chew.

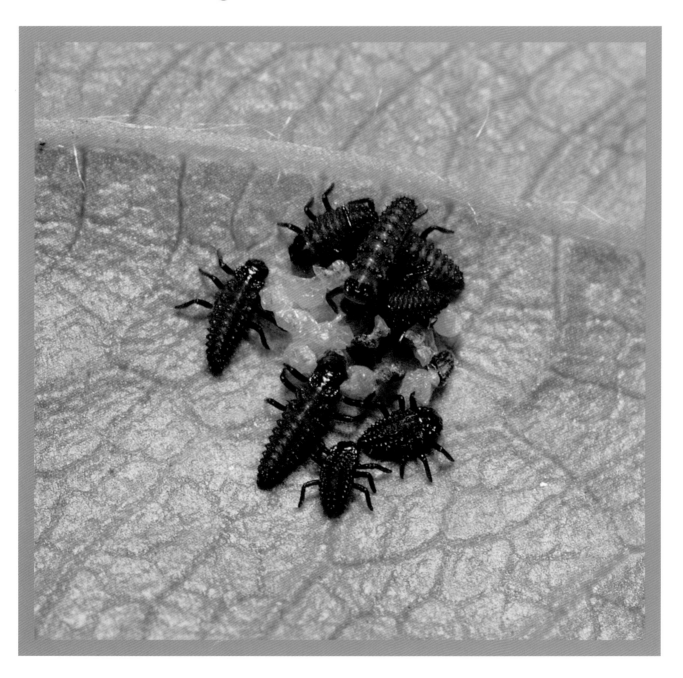

The larva looks for food.

Two days after leaving its egg, the **larva** crawls away to look for food. If it cannot find something to eat quickly, it will often eat another larva.

Ladybird larvae live alone. They are great **hunters**. They use their six strong legs to climb over plants and seek out and eat other **insects**.

The larva eats mostly aphids.

The **larva** eats mostly green **aphids**. Aphids damage garden plants so the larvae are helpful to gardeners.

A larva is always hungry. One larva can eat over 30 aphids a day. It uses its sharp jaws to grab an aphid. It chews it and sucks out all the juice, leaving behind an empty aphid skin.

The larva grows.

The **larva** eats so many **aphids** that it has to shed its skin to grow bigger.

When this happens, the larva attaches itself to a leaf. After a day its skin splits and the larva crawls out, leaving the old skin behind. A larva changes its skin three times before it is fully grown.

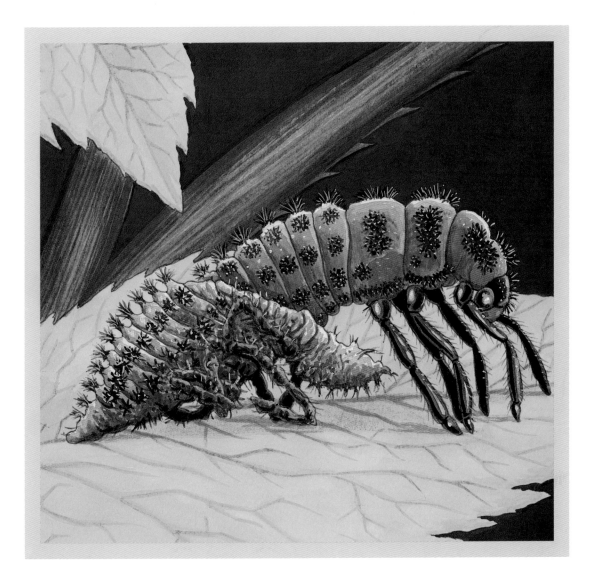

The larva is fully grown.

After two weeks the **larva**
is fully grown.

It finds a safe place, such as the underside of a leaf. It sticks itself to the leaf with a special glue from its rear end, and spends the next day hunched up. Inside its skin, it is changing into a **pupa**.

The larva becomes a pupa.

Four days later, the **larva** skin splits and a **pupa** wriggles out. The pupa case is soft at first, but it hardens after a day.

As the pupa hardens, it changes colour and looks like a bird dropping. This stops **predators** from eating it. After a week the pupa darkens.

The ladybird leaves the pupa.

Two weeks later, a ladybird starts to push its way out of the **pupa** case. The case splits and an adult ladybird struggles out.

The ladybird uses hooks on the end of its legs to cling to the leaf and pull itself out. Its body is weak, so it just rests. It cannot fly or eat until its body is dry and its wings are strong.

The ladybird gets its spots.

The ladybird's wings are protected by its wing cases. At first the ladybird's wing cases are yellow-orange without any spots.

As the ladybird's body hardens, the spots slowly appear and the wing cases turn red. This takes about two days. The ladybird keeps its wings folded until it needs them to fly.

The ladybird flies.

The ladybird can only fly when the weather is warm. Its wing **muscles** need warmth in order to work properly.

A ladybird is too heavy to take off. Instead it climbs a plant stem or a blade of grass to help it. When it is ready to fly the ladybird unfolds its wings from under the wing cases and flies away.

The ladybird feeds.

The adult ladybird is a **hunter**, just like the larva. It eats **aphids**, and flies from plant to plant looking for them.

A female ladybird will eat up to 100 aphids a day before she starts to lay eggs, and up to 5,000 during her lifetime. She needs a lot of food to help the eggs develop.

The ladybird mates.

After a week, the ladybird looks for a mate. The male clings to the female's back and transfers his **sperm** to her.

Afterwards, the male flies off to
find another female. A female
ladybird only mates once. A day or
two later, she looks for a plant
with **aphids**, and lays her eggs
nearby. When they hatch, the
larvae will be close to their
favourite food.

Word bank

Aphids - Tiny insects that live off plants. They are the main source of food for ladybirds.

Batches - A set amount of something that has been got ready. You can have a batch of bread or a batch of eggs.

Hunter - A hunter chases or searches for other animals to eat.

Insects - A creature with six legs, a pair of wings and two eyes.

Larva or larvae - After ladybirds hatch they live as larvae until they grow their skin and wings. Larvae look like maggots or grains of rice.

Muscles - Tissues that help animals and insects to carry heavy objects and move around.

Predators - Animals that hunt and eat other animals. A ladybird is a predator of small insects.

Pupa - The stage an insect goes through as it changes from larva to adult. It has soft skin and no wings.

Sperm - The male cells needed to fertilise eggs.

Life cycle

Five days after the eggs
are laid ladybird larvae
crawl out.

The ladybird is ready
to mate and the female
lays eggs.

Two days later,
the larvae
move away.

A larva eats so much
that it needs to shed
its skin.

Slowly the ladybird's spots appear
and the wing cases turn red.

Two weeks later the pupa has
changed into a ladybird.

After two weeks the larva
is fully grown.

Four days later, the
skin splits and a
pupa crawls out.

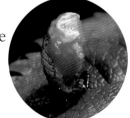

Index